Copyright © Samuel karanja, 2024

All rights reserved. No part of this book may be reproduced, stored in a retrieval system, or transmitted in any form or by any means, electronic, mechanical, photocopying, recording, scanning, or otherwise, without the prior written permission of the publisher, except as permitted by copyright law.

Table of Contents

1. Introduction: A Call to Action
2. Embracing Change: The Power of Adaptability
3. Defining Success: Finding Your True North
4. Overcoming Fear: Courage in the Face of Adversity
5. Building Resilience: Bouncing Back Stronger
6. The Growth Mindset: Cultivating a Positive Outlook
7. Finding Purpose: Discovering Your Why
8. Goal Setting: Charting Your Course for Success
9. Time Management: Maximizing Your Productivity
10. Effective Communication: Mastering the Art of Connection
11. Building Relationships: The Foundation of Success

12. Financial Literacy: Navigating the Path to Wealth
13. Leadership Principles: Guiding Others to Greatness
14. Innovation and Creativity: Thinking Outside the Box
15. Personal Branding: Crafting Your Unique Identity
16. Celebrating Heroes: Honoring Those Who Inspire
17. Flow, Not Force: Surrendering to Your Life's Calling
18. Conclusion: Embracing Your Journey

Introduction:

Welcome, dear reader, to a journey of transformation and empowerment. In the pages that follow, you will embark on a voyage of self-discovery, guided by the wisdom and insights of Vusi Thembenkwayo, a beacon of inspiration in the realm of personal and professional development.

In today's fast-paced and ever-changing world, the pursuit of success can often feel like an elusive quest. We find ourselves navigating through a maze of challenges, uncertainties, and obstacles, unsure of which path to take or how to overcome the hurdles in our way. Yet, amidst the chaos and confusion, there exists a beacon of hope—a vision of possibility and potential waiting to be realized.

Vusi Thembenkwayo is no stranger to adversity. Born and raised in the townships of South Africa during the tumultuous era of apartheid, he rose above his circumstances to become a renowned entrepreneur, speaker, and thought leader. His journey from humble beginnings to global success is a testament to the power of resilience, determination, and unwavering belief in oneself.

In this book, Vusi shares with you the principles, strategies, and mindset shifts that have propelled him to greatness. Drawing upon his own experiences and insights gained from years of navigating the highs and lows of entrepreneurship, he offers practical advice and actionable steps to help you unleash your full potential and achieve your goals.

Whether you're a seasoned business leader, an aspiring

entrepreneur, or simply someone striving for personal growth and fulfillment, the lessons contained within these pages will inspire you to dream bigger, reach higher, and live your best life. So, let us embark together on this journey of discovery, as we unlock the secrets to success and unleash the power within.

The time for transformation is now. Are you ready to unleash your potential?

Chapter 1:

The Unexpected Approach

In the quiet hours of a South African night, a young man sought guidance from a mentor. Their conversation sparked a tale of daring and ingenuity, one that would forever change the way we perceive making an impression.

It began with a simple plea: "There's this beautiful girl," the young man confessed, "and I've been trying to get her attention on Instagram." Little did he know, his quest for affection would unveil a strategy that transcends romance, a strategy rooted in the art of making an impression.

As the mentor listened, he recognized an opportunity to impart wisdom. "Let's play the odds," he proposed. For in a world of endless admirers, how does one stand out? The answer lay not in conformity but in creativity.

Thus, a plan was devised—a message, not of flattery, but of curiosity. "Where should I send it?" the young man wrote, leaving the recipient intrigued, if not perplexed. And in the digital realm where attention is fleeting, curiosity is the currency of engagement.

What transpired next was nothing short of miraculous. A reply, a question, a dialogue initiated by the simplest of inquiries. "Just GPS me your address," the young man boldly declared, defying convention with confidence.

In that moment, a connection was forged—not through hollow compliments or rehearsed lines, but through authenticity and originality. And as the conversation unfolded, it became clear that this was more than a love story; it was a lesson in the art of making an impression.

For in every interaction, whether seeking romance or opportunity, there exists a choice—to blend into the background or to stand out with purpose. And though the path may be uncertain, the rewards are reserved for those willing to embrace the unexpected.

As the mentor concluded his tale, he imparted a truth that transcends circumstance: "Whether you're seeking an investor or recruiting talent, the key lies in differentiation. It's not about being like everyone else; it's about being uniquely you."

And so, the journey begins—a journey fueled by curiosity, guided by creativity, and defined by the courage to defy expectations. For in the art of making an impression, the possibilities are as limitless as the imagination.

Join us as we explore the stories and strategies that shape success, where every encounter is an opportunity, and every impression is a masterpiece in the making. Welcome to The Art of Making an Impression.

Chapter 2:

The Effort of Doing Something Big

In the grand tapestry of entrepreneurship, each thread represents a unique journey—a saga of trials, triumphs, and transformation. As our story unfolds, we find ourselves immersed in the narrative of a determined entrepreneur, whose quest for success transcends the ordinary.

In the bustling landscape of modern romance, our protagonist's journey begins—a digital odyssey fraught with challenges and opportunities. Like every suitor vying for attention in the crowded realm of social media, our entrepreneur endeavors to capture the heart of his audience, to stand out amidst the noise and clamor.

Yet, amidst the pursuit of connection, a profound truth emerges—the belief that one is the best option available. Just as every admirer believes himself to be the epitome of desirability, so too does our entrepreneur strive to position himself as the premier choice in his industry.

But the path to success is fraught with obstacles, as our protagonist soon discovers. Navigating the intricacies of business dealings and contractual obligations, he confronts the harsh reality of entrepreneurship—a world where uncertainty reigns supreme, and adversity lurks around every corner.

Amidst the chaos and uncertainty, however, a guiding principle emerges—a beacon of hope amidst the storm. It is the understanding that the effort it takes to do something big is no different from the effort it takes to do something small—that in every setback lies the seed of opportunity, waiting to be nurtured and cultivated.

As our protagonist grapples with the challenges of lease agreements and insurance products, he realizes the importance of mindset—the unwavering belief in his own potential, even in the face of adversity. For in the journey of entrepreneurship, it is not merely knowledge or experience that sustains us, but the resilience of the human spirit.

And so, our protagonist presses onward, undeterred by the trials and tribulations that lie ahead. For in the pursuit of greatness, every obstacle is but a stepping stone on the path to success, every setback a lesson to be learned and overcome.

As the chapter draws to a close, our protagonist stands poised on the brink of discovery, ready to face whatever challenges lie ahead. For in the grand adventure of entrepreneurship, the effort it takes to do something big is the same effort it takes to do something small—and every step forward brings us closer to our dreams.

Join us as we embark on a journey of discovery—a voyage into the heart of entrepreneurship, where the pursuit of greatness knows no bounds, and the human spirit soars to new heights. Welcome to The

Entrepreneur's Odyssey: Navigating Adversity to Achieve Greatness.

Chapter 3:

Unveiling the Science of Communication

"Hello, family, hey guys, I wanted to uh come into your space today, uh to share the following with you, so the single most important gift in the world, in my mind, is the gift of communication, the greatest tool of influence." These were the opening words of a conversation that would unravel the secrets of persuasion and influence—a journey into the heart of effective communication.

In the realm of leadership, communication reigns supreme. It is the cornerstone upon which great leaders build their legacies, the driving force behind every significant achievement. Without effective communication, influence becomes an elusive dream, a distant mirage in the desert of ambition.

"All leaders have is communication. You cannot influence where you cannot communicate; it's impossible." These words echoed with undeniable truth, resonating deeply with those who aspired to lead. For in the arena of leadership, the ability to communicate with clarity and conviction is the catalyst for change, the spark that ignites the flames of progress.

But communication alone is not enough; it must be wielded with purpose and intent. "So learning to communicate is a critical skill for any of you who think of yourselves as leaders," emphasized the speaker. "But if you would learn to communicate, the question becomes: communicate for what purpose? What's the outcome?"

Indeed, the purpose of communication is twofold—to inspire action and to reshape perspectives. Whether rallying a team to achieve a common goal or challenging the status quo, effective communication is the linchpin of success. "The reason we human beings communicate is to either get somebody to do something we want them to do or to get somebody to see something we want them to see," the speaker explained.

Yet, the art of persuasion extends far beyond the realm of salesmanship. "Sales at the end of the day is how you transact; it's how I get you to not only see value but take action on the value that you see," the speaker elucidated. "Persuasion, though, is a broader science."

As the conversation unfolded, the speaker delved into the intricacies of persuasion, unveiling its underlying principles. "It's actually scientific," he proclaimed. "There is a process you can follow, and if you follow the process, you'll get the outcome."

The first step on the path to mastery, he explained, is to understand motivations. "Everybody does something because everybody wants something; we're human beings, we're creatures of incentive," he declared. By delving into the implicit motivations of others, one gains insight into their desires and aspirations—a crucial element of effective persuasion.

Intent, the speaker argued, is equally vital. "Intent is what impact do they want to have, their true intent, their motive, their um, the outcome they desire," he elucidated. By aligning one's message with the desired impact of their audience, they increase the likelihood of success.

Central to the art of persuasion is the ability to articulate a compelling vision—a just cause that resonates with the hearts and minds of others. "The cause has to be a just cause," the speaker emphasized. "People have to believe that the cause is worth pursuing."

Illustrating his point with a real-life example, the speaker recounted a conversation with a potential recruit. By appealing to her sense of purpose and offering a vision of a brighter future, he sought to inspire her to join their cause—a cause greater than any individual ambition.

As the chapter drew to a close, the speaker's passion was palpable. "I'm on fire right now; I know, I know," he exclaimed. For in the pursuit of effective communication lies the power to inspire, to influence, and to lead—a power that knows no bounds.

Join us in the next chapter as we explore the practical applications of persuasion, from boardrooms to living rooms, and discover the transformative potential of mastering the art of communication.

Chapter 4:

The Pitfalls and Solutions of Rapid Growth

In the journey of entrepreneurship, the allure of rapid growth often blinds us to its inherent challenges. The exhilaration of soaring revenues can mask the underlying fragility of our cash flow. In this chapter, we'll delve into the telltale signs of a business growing too fast and explore strategies to navigate this perilous terrain.

Signs of Overwhelming Growth:

Imagine receiving a flurry of orders, each one promising exponential revenue growth. It's a dream scenario, right? But hold on, let's look beneath the surface. 30 days after shipping the orders, you send out invoices, anticipating a healthy cash influx. However, reality hits hard when 90 days pass, and your bank balance remains stagnant. This scenario is not uncommon in the world of business. The apparent success of soaring revenues can often mask the underlying cash crunch.

Understanding the Cash Flow Mirage:

The allure of high turnover figures can be deceptive. Picture this: you receive a substantial order, and you're elated. You log it as turnover, projecting a rosy financial picture to investors. But here's the catch – until those invoices are paid, they're merely promissory notes, not cash in hand. Your business may appear cash-rich on paper, but in reality, it's starved of liquidity.

Addressing Working Capital Woes:

As customer complaints start piling up, it's a red flag signaling operational strain. A fivefold increase in complaints within a short span is a clear indicator of system overload. It's a symptom of outgrowing your existing infrastructure. Additionally, working capital problems rear their head as invoices remain unpaid, tying up crucial funds needed for day-to-day operations.

Strategies for Sustainable Growth:

So, what's the solution? The first step is acknowledging the problem and seeking external support. Fintech companies offer innovative solutions, providing upfront cash against outstanding invoices. While it may seem counterintuitive to accept less than the full invoice amount, the immediate liquidity ensures business continuity.

Building a Robust Support System:

Ultimately, success lies in the quality of your team. Surround yourself with individuals who can navigate the complexities of rapid growth. Retailers have mastered this art, leveraging financial maneuvers to optimize cash flow. By adopting a similar approach, you can mitigate the risks of overzealous expansion.

Embracing Strategic Partnerships:

When venturing into new markets, partnerships can be your saving grace. Rather than shouldering the execution risk alone, collaborate with local partners who understand the nuances of the market. This minimizes exposure while maximizing potential returns.

Moving Beyond Criticism:

In the broader context of economic development, Africa stands at a crossroads. While criticism may highlight shortcomings, action is the catalyst for change. It's time to move beyond rhetoric and embrace proactive strategies for growth. Let's chart a course that empowers African businesses to shape their destiny on the global stage.

Conclusion:

Navigating rapid growth requires foresight, adaptability, and strategic planning. By recognizing the warning signs, seeking external support, and fostering robust partnerships, entrepreneurs can build resilient businesses capable of withstanding the challenges of scaling. Let's embark on this journey together, armed with the knowledge and determination to succeed in an ever-evolving marketplace.

Chapter 5:

Understanding the Monogamous Relationship Between Capital and Return

In the realm of wealth accumulation and financial management, the dynamics between capital and return play a pivotal role. As I often tell people, capital maintains a supremely monogamous relationship with return, akin to a steadfast commitment that transcends ideologies and social pressures. This unwavering fidelity of capital to seek out the highest return forms the cornerstone of economic decision-making.

The Temptation of Quick Wealth and Its Pitfalls:

Individuals who amass wealth rapidly often find themselves ensnared in a cycle of lavish spending and eventual financial ruin. The allure of easy money can breed complacency, leading to a misguided belief that the coffers will never run dry. However, this mindset overlooks the fundamental principle that capital will always gravitate towards the most lucrative opportunities, regardless of personal aspirations or societal ideals.

Differentiating Between Riches and Old Money:

In the pursuit of wealth, one must discern between ostentatious displays of riches and the understated elegance of old money. While the nouveau riche flaunt their newfound fortunes through extravagant purchases and boastful announcements, those with a legacy of wealth embody humility and discretion. Old money eschews the need for validation, preferring to quietly steward their resources for future generations.

Navigating the Pitfalls of Sudden Wealth:

For young entrepreneurs catapulted into the limelight by viral success or sudden windfalls, the journey from rags to riches can be perilous. The allure of newfound wealth often clouds judgment, leading to reckless spending and financial mismanagement. The key lies in understanding the aggregation of wealth over time and embracing a disciplined approach to long-term financial planning.

Strategies for Sustainable Wealth Management:

To avoid the pitfalls of squandered wealth, individuals must adopt a mindset of prudent aggregation. Rather than viewing wealth as a finite sum to be depleted, consider it as a resource to be carefully allocated over a lifetime. By incorporating principles of compound growth and prudent investment, one can safeguard against the erosion of purchasing power and ensure financial security for the future.

Empowering the Next Generation of Wealth Stewards:

Aspiring entrepreneurs and wealth creators must heed the lessons of history and eschew the trappings of fleeting success. By cultivating a culture of financial literacy and long-term thinking, we can empower the next generation to chart a course towards sustainable prosperity. Through mentorship, education, and a commitment to prudent stewardship, we can transcend the allure of quick riches and build a legacy of enduring wealth for generations to come.

Conclusion:

In the intricate dance between capital and return, the path to enduring wealth is paved with prudence, discipline, and foresight. By embracing the principles of sustainable wealth management and eschewing the allure of fleeting riches, individuals can navigate the complexities of financial success with grace and resilience. Let us embark on this journey together, mindful of the timeless wisdom that capital, like a faithful companion, will always seek out the highest return, provided we steer its course with wisdom and discernment.

Chapter 6:

Unmasking the Web of Deception: How to Spot and Avoid Online Scammers

In the ever-expanding digital landscape, where connectivity knows no bounds, the rise of online scams has become an unfortunate reality. Foreign scammers, cloaked in anonymity, are preying on unsuspecting individuals with promises of love and wealth, only to strip them of their hard-earned money. This chapter serves as a beacon of awareness, shedding light on the insidious tactics employed by these perpetrators and equipping you with the knowledge to protect yourself against their schemes.

The Genesis of Deception:

The tale begins with a disheartening revelation—the nefarious infiltration of social media platforms by imposters masquerading as reputable figures. These imposters, armed with stolen identities and fabricated personas, weave intricate webs of deceit, enticing victims with false promises of investment opportunities and romantic endeavors. The proliferation of fake profiles and counterfeit communications serves as the initial warning sign of an impending scam.

Unveiling the Red Flags:

Amidst the sea of digital interactions, discerning the authentic from the fraudulent requires a keen eye and a vigilant spirit. Several red flags serve as beacons of caution in the treacherous waters of online communication:

1. **Punctuation Perils:** Scammers often reveal their true colors through their careless disregard for proper punctuation and grammar. A discerning eye can easily spot inconsistencies and errors in their written

communication, serving as an immediate indicator of fraudulent intent.
2. **Verification Vigilance:** Verification badges and community size serve as crucial indicators of legitimacy in the online realm. Genuine individuals and reputable entities boast verified accounts and substantial followings, providing a shield against impersonators and imposters.
3. **Name Game:** Scrutinizing the spelling and authenticity of names can uncover the facade of deceit woven by scammers. Utilizing search engines to cross-reference names and profiles ensures that you're interacting with the genuine article, rather than a cunning impersonator.
4. **Image Integrity:** Harnessing the power of reverse image search unveils the true identity behind masked profiles. By verifying the authenticity of images and profiles, you safeguard yourself against falling prey to counterfeit personas and fabricated narratives.
5. **Emotional Exploitation:** Scammers exploit human emotions, leveraging words of encouragement and empathy to manipulate their victims. Beware of unsolicited messages laden with emotional

appeals, as they often serve as the precursor to a fraudulent scheme.

The Cryptocurrency Conundrum:

In the realm of online fraud, cryptocurrencies have emerged as the currency of choice for scammers seeking to evade detection. The anonymity afforded by cryptocurrency transactions renders victims powerless in the face of deception, amplifying the urgency of remaining vigilant against suspicious solicitations.

Taking a Stand Against Fraud:

Armed with the knowledge of deception's anatomy, it falls upon each individual to take a stand against online fraud. By reporting suspicious activity to the appropriate authorities and educating others about the perils of digital deception, we can collectively combat the scourge of online scams.

Conclusion:

As the digital landscape continues to evolve, so too must our vigilance in safeguarding against online scams. By heeding the warning signs, verifying the authenticity of online interactions, and fostering a culture of awareness, we can fortify ourselves against the insidious schemes of online scammers. Let us stand united in the fight against fraud, ensuring that the digital realm remains a safe and secure space for all.

Chapter 7:

Understanding the Problem to Find the Solution

So, what have we covered here today? Well, let's dive into it. The first thing we discussed was the fundamental difference between management and leadership. But as we delved deeper, we realized that the world has evolved. It's no longer just about the marketplace, the product, or the customer. Everything now exists on a platform. Our value, as individuals focused on customers and markets, lies in the intimacy and connection we bring to the market we serve. However, there's a crucial missing piece: converting this knowledge into a language that our stakeholders can understand.

Understanding Operating Leverage: A Financial Perspective

Imagine sitting down with a finance person like my friend Donald, and discussing whether to open a new store or invest in an online platform. In finance and management accounting, we use a measure called the degree of operating leverage (DOL) to assess the leverage an additional unit of activity provides. The DOL is calculated by dividing the contribution margin by the net operating income. Let's break it down further.

Contributing to the Conversation: The Big D Coffee Business

Donald and I decide to start a coffee business called "The Big D." We contemplate opening a new store or launching an online platform. If we open a new store, we need to consider fixed and variable costs. However, with an online platform, the only costs are the ingredients. The key is understanding the contribution margin: revenue minus variable costs.

Applying Financial Insights to Decision Making

The discussion between Donald and me isn't about mere options but about which strategy offers a higher DOL. This conversation applies beyond coffee shops. It's about demonstrating to stakeholders how we can leverage existing infrastructure to maximize returns. Whether you're a startup founder or a marketing team seeking investment, framing your proposal in terms of DOL can be compelling.

Reframing Problems to Find Solutions

Consider McDonald's and Shake Shack. McDonald's, born in the era of mass production and efficiency, thrives on speed and efficiency rather than culinary excellence. But in today's world, consumers seek more than just fast food; they demand quality and nutritional value. McDonald's recognized this shift and adapted by offering healthier options.

Questioning Assumptions and Embracing Innovation

The key takeaway? Don't be married to your initial problem-solving assumptions. Innovate by continuously questioning what problem you're truly solving. Innovation lies in the pursuit of problems seeking solutions. So, ask yourself: What problem are you solving? And who told you that was the real problem?

Embracing the Journey of Discovery

In the end, it's about falling in love with the process of understanding and solving problems. Just as my brother Julian highlighted, many startups fail because they realize they're solving the wrong problem. True innovation comes from the relentless pursuit of understanding the real problem and finding the solution that truly addresses it. So, keep asking, keep exploring, and keep innovating.

Chapter 8:

Unveiling the Illusion

nerves prickling beneath the surface, I can't help but be reminded of the rhythmic beats of Gillan's music echoing in the background. It's a reminder of the diverse tapestry that makes up our society, yet also a reflection of the cultural divides that still linger.

Reflecting on my own journey, I recall the days when I began speaking professionally, clad in suits and All-Stars, a symbol of both aspiration and heritage. Each step I took was a testament to where I was headed, yet rooted in the humble origins that shaped me.

But beyond the personal anecdotes lies a deeper truth—a truth about the power dynamics at play in our society. The creator of Facebook, a platform that connects billions worldwide, remains oblivious to the existence of each individual in this room. It's a stark contrast to the American ethos, where children are taught to think and build for the global community, while we confine ourselves to local concerns.

Yet, despite the knowledge we've gained, we remain entrenched in the status quo, content to cling to familiar comforts. We believe ourselves united in our desires, but the truth is, we are divided. What our country truly needs from us is not just action, but faith—the ability to envision the invisible, believe in the impossible, and trust in the unknown.

As we delve into the stories of two intriguing businesses—Juan's Lotion Culture and Mr. Price—we uncover the disparities that exist despite similar beginnings. What sets one apart from the other? And why does Tebow's Puzzle Shop struggle while Quarter Joe's thrives?

The answer lies in our understanding of power—the power within each of us to effect change. From humble stock fells to billion-rand banking institutions, the principles remain the same. Yet, somewhere along the way, we've been fed a lie—a lie that small businesses are the key to success, yet they remain stagnant, unable to disrupt the status quo.

I reflect on my own grandfather's journey, starting a puzzle shop in 1978 with hopes of prosperity. Despite his efforts, he passed away with only one shop to his name. Meanwhile, young entrepreneurs in Stellenbosch were gathering, laying the groundwork for future success.

It's time to unveil the illusion that has held us back for far too long. It's time to recognize our own power and potential—to disrupt, to innovate, and to build a future that transcends the confines of the status quo. **Chapter 8: Breaking the Chains of Small Thinking**

In the annals of entrepreneurial history, there lies a tale of two beginnings: one, a humble puzzle shop launched by my grandfather in 1978; the other, the birth of Shoprite by Chris - and his cohorts, who pooled their resources and ambitions into a venture that would soon soar. While my grandfather's aspirations remained modest, Shoprite burgeoned into a behemoth, raking in billions in turnover.

But what sets these two narratives apart? Beyond the surface lies a profound truth—a truth about the shackles of small thinking that have ensnared us for generations. While systemic oppression aimed to keep us disenfranchised, its greatest victory was instilling in us the belief that smallness was not only acceptable but preferable.

This insidious belief permeates our education systems, our businesses, and our collective consciousness. How often do we witness aspiring entrepreneurs embarking on their journey, only to remain trapped in the confines of mediocrity? We register our businesses, chase tenders, and measure success by the narrowest of metrics, all the while failing to realize our true potential.

The solution lies not in complacency but in upheaval—in dismantling the very foundations upon which our small-mindedness rests. If we are to confront the scourge of unemployment, particularly among our youth, we must challenge the status quo with unwavering resolve.

It is imperative that we transcend the confines of startup culture and embrace the full spectrum of entrepreneurial endeavors. From the solitary startup founder to the ostentatious success entrepreneur, we must recognize that true progress lies in the realm of hyper-growth entrepreneurship.

These rare individuals, driven by a long-term vision and a commitment to education, hold the key to our collective prosperity. They eschew the trappings of superficial success in favor of meaningful impact, leveraging their networks not for personal gain but for the greater good.

In my encounters with entrepreneurs like Dough Balls, I am reminded of the transformative power of ambition unleashed. Despite modest beginnings, these growth entrepreneurs possess an innate understanding of their industries, coupled with a hunger for change that transcends personal ambition.

As I reflect on my experiences on Dragon's Den, I am struck by the stark contrast between small thinkers and visionaries. From Mr. President's dubious theories to the audacious dreams of hyper-growth entrepreneurs, the divide is palpable.

But amidst the cacophony of voices, there is one constant—a profound sense of resilience that defines us as a people. Whether greeting each other with a nod or speaking in the language of numbers, we possess a resilience that transcends adversity.

It is this resilience, this refusal to be confined by the limitations of small thinking, that will propel us forward into a future of boundless opportunity. As we cast off the chains of mediocrity and embrace the audacity of our dreams, we pave the way for a brighter, more prosperous South Africa.

The third aspect is the need for a robust ecosystem that fosters innovation and collaboration. We cannot expect entrepreneurs to thrive in isolation; they need a supportive network of resources, partnerships, and opportunities to flourish. This includes access to funding, mentorship, training programs, and platforms for collaboration.

Furthermore, we must cultivate a culture of risk-taking and resilience. Entrepreneurship is inherently risky, but it is also the engine of progress and innovation. We need to celebrate failure as a stepping stone to success and provide aspiring entrepreneurs with the tools and support they need to bounce back from setbacks.

Finally, we must prioritize inclusivity and diversity in entrepreneurship. Too often, certain demographics are excluded or marginalized in the entrepreneurial ecosystem. We need to break down barriers and create opportunities for all people, regardless of race, gender, or background, to participate and thrive in the economy.

In essence, building a thriving entrepreneurial ecosystem requires a multifaceted approach that addresses infrastructure, mindset, support systems, and inclusivity. By investing in these areas, we can unlock the full potential of South Africa's entrepreneurs and pave the way for a brighter, more prosperous future. That was quite a powerful and thought-provoking presentation! It seems like the speaker covered a wide range of topics, from the importance of delayed gratification to the biases that influence our decision-making processes. Here are some key takeaways:

1. **Delayed Gratification**: The speaker emphasized the need to cultivate a culture of delayed gratification, where individuals are willing to wait for opportunities and resist the temptation for instant rewards. This mindset can be crucial for long-term success and achievement.

2. **Conspicuous Consumption**: The speaker discussed the phenomenon of conspicuous consumption, where individuals feel the need to flaunt their wealth and possessions to impress others. This mindset can lead to financial mismanagement and hinder entrepreneurial success.

3. **Business Plans**: The speaker challenged the traditional notion of writing business plans, arguing that they are often outdated by the time they are completed. Instead, entrepreneurs should focus on taking action, learning from mistakes, and adapting quickly to changing market conditions.

4. **Confirmation Bias and Status Quo Bias**: The speaker highlighted how these cognitive biases influence our perception of information and our resistance to change. Understanding and overcoming these biases is essential for making informed decisions and embracing innovation.

5. **Unity and Faith**: The speaker concluded by emphasizing the importance of unity and faith in building a better future for South Africa. Despite political divisions, all citizens share common aspirations for a safer, more prosperous country.

Overall, the presentation seems to have encouraged introspection and reflection on both individual and societal levels, urging listeners to challenge conventional thinking and take proactive steps towards positive change.

Chapter 9:

Dealing with Business Failures

It's curious, isn't it? When you speak to anyone working with business owners and founders, they'll likely recount the high rate of business failures within the initial phases. Whether it's the first 12 months, the first 24 months, or stretching to the first 36 months, the failure rates are often alarmingly high, reaching double digits. Despite varied data and limited evidence, it's clear that the survival rate for early-stage companies is precarious.

Yet, amidst these statistics, one glaring absence stands out: where are the books teaching entrepreneurs how to fail? We're inundated with guides on how to start and grow a business, but very little guidance exists on navigating failure when it inevitably strikes. Every entrepreneur, sooner or later, encounters what can be described as a near-death experience (NDE) for their business.

It took my own NDE to prompt a realization: there's a lack of resources addressing what to do when things go wrong. In such moments, reaching out to mentors and experienced individuals became paramount. Here's what I learned and what I believe can offer guidance to entrepreneurs facing turbulent times:

Firstly, educate yourself. Understand the laws governing businesses in your country. Know the responsibilities and duties of directors, including fiduciary duties and obligations during insolvency.

Secondly, secure the expertise of a top-notch corporate lawyer, preferably one experienced in liquidations. This isn't the time for sales promotions or marketing strategies; it's about protecting yourself legally.

Thirdly, consult with your accountant to assess the financial health of your business. Are you receiving timely financial statements? Are you aware of the going concern status of your company?

Next, tread cautiously. Operating a business on the brink of collapse can have legal ramifications. Understand the implications of trading recklessly and seek advice on how to proceed ethically and legally.

Finally, consider stepping down from your role as the leader of your company. Entrust the operations to someone else, someone less emotionally invested and more capable of making objective decisions. It's a tough pill to swallow, but it could be the best decision for the long-term survival of your business.

This advice may not be popular or easy to follow, but it's grounded in reality. It's the tough, grown-up advice that many entrepreneurs need when facing the harsh realities of business failure. And if even one person finds solace and guidance in this message, then its purpose has been fulfilled.

Chapter 10:

Embracing Where You Are

There's a particular moment that stands out in my memory, a moment where envy threatened to overwhelm me. It was during a meeting with three individuals who had invited me to join them in a business venture. As they outlined their plans and discussed their successes, I couldn't help but feel a pang of regret for not being involved. Yet, despite the temptation to dwell on what could have been, I reminded myself that I am exactly where I'm supposed to be.

Let me share a bit of background. About a year ago, I was presented with an opportunity to join this venture. However, my schedule was already packed with commitments, and I simply didn't have the bandwidth to take on something new. Even now, my plate remains full with various projects and responsibilities.

So I declined the offer, and these three individuals went ahead with their plans. As I later discovered, they achieved remarkable success in a remarkably short period. Hearing about their accomplishments filled me with envy. If envy had the power to transform me, I would have left that meeting resembling the Hulk.

But despite my fleeting regret, I realized something profound: I am exactly where I'm supposed to be. This realization is empowering because it shifts the focus from dwelling on missed opportunities to embracing the lessons and growth inherent in my current situation.

Jeff Bezos once spoke about the "regret minimization matrix," a framework for decision-making based on minimizing future regrets rather than maximizing immediate gains. It's a concept that resonated with me as I reflected on my own choices. While I may have missed out on certain opportunities, I'm grateful for the path I've chosen to follow.

In a moment of clarity, I recognized that my character is defined not solely by the decisions I make, but by the commitment and follow-through I exhibit. Despite any regrets I may harbor, I've remained steadfast in pursuing the endeavors that align with my long-term goals.

Moreover, I've come to appreciate the resilience and perseverance required to navigate the challenges of entrepreneurship. It's not easy to sustain oneself through periods of uncertainty and financial instability. Yet, by staying true to my vision and dedicating myself to the tasks at hand, I've continued to progress toward my objectives.

If you find yourself grappling with regrets or longing for a different path, I encourage you to consider this: You are exactly where you're supposed to be. Embrace this truth and ask yourself what lessons you can glean from your current circumstances.

Reflect on the decisions that led you here and identify areas for growth and improvement. Remember, the best lessons often emerge from the most challenging experiences. Use these lessons to propel yourself forward and chart a course toward your desired destination.

Imagine your life as a movie, with you as the main character. If this moment were the opening scene, how would you want the rest of the story to unfold? Take inspiration from your own narrative and envision the hero's journey that lies ahead.

Yes, it may sound idealistic, but it's grounded in a simple truth: Do the hard things, and the rest will fall into place. So, embrace the challenges, learn from the setbacks, and trust that you are exactly where you need to be on your journey to success.

This isn't about wishful thinking; it's about taking decisive action and persevering through adversity. So, go ahead, be your own superhero, and write the next chapter of your story with courage and determination.

Remember, it's through the hardships that we discover our true strength and resilience. So, embrace the journey, and let your story unfold with purpose and conviction.

Chapter 11:

Reflections on Authentic Connection

Hello, family. If you're familiar with the VT Podcast, you'll recognize the reference, so let's dive in. This is an impromptu message, spurred by a thought that demanded to be shared. Amidst the hustle and bustle of life, there are countless individuals grappling with their own struggles.

Allow me to share a personal story. When I was just 19 years old, I experienced the profound loss of my best friend. Clyde and I had been inseparable since our high school days, sharing jokes and dreams. He was a vibrant soul, always ready with a smile and a word of encouragement. His sudden departure left me shattered, grappling with the unanswered question: why?

Clyde's passing forced me to confront the stark reality of our human experience. Too often, we wear masks, projecting a facade of happiness while concealing our inner turmoil. It's only in moments of tragedy that we yearn for genuine connection, for someone to ask, "Are you okay?" with sincerity.

I've had my own moments of vulnerability, times when I questioned whether I could overcome the challenges life threw my way. Despite my achievements, I too have faced moments of doubt and insecurity. The pressure to live up to others' expectations weighed heavily on me, threatening to erode my sense of self.

Yet, in the face of adversity, I found solace in authenticity. I realized that true strength lies in vulnerability, in the willingness to acknowledge our struggles and seek support. It's easy to succumb to the allure of negativity, to lash out at others from behind the safety of a screen. But true kindness requires empathy, a genuine concern for the well-being of others.

As a South African, I'm keenly aware of the recent passing of influential figures like King Yokozi and Ricky Rick. Their untimely deaths serve as a sobering reminder of life's fragility. Every moment is precious, every interaction an opportunity to uplift and inspire.

So, I implore you to pause and reflect on the impact of your words and actions. Are you contributing to a culture of kindness and understanding, or are you perpetuating negativity and divisiveness? Each of us has the power to shape the world around us, to leave a legacy of compassion and empathy.

In times of darkness, it's crucial to lean on faith and community for support. While I may not have all the answers, I find comfort in knowing that I am not alone in my journey. Together, we can create a world where authenticity reigns supreme, where kindness is the currency of connection.

So, as you go about your day, remember to be kind—to yourself and to others. In a world fraught with challenges, your kindness may be the beacon of hope someone desperately needs. Let's strive to leave every interaction a little brighter than we found it, for therein lies the true measure of our humanity.

Cheers, and may you find peace and fulfillment on your journey.

Chapter 12:

Trusting the Instrumentation

So, recently, I found myself on tour in Namibia, soaking in the beauty of the landscape and the warmth of its people. One particular highlight was a journey to a lodge nestled in the desert, a place of serene majesty. Yet, the journey itself offered a profound lesson in trust and navigation.

As we embarked on our return flight from the desert to Ventok, we boarded a small Cessna plane, navigating through mountainous terrain. Turbulence shook the cabin, and my nerves were on edge. However, what unfolded next left me both puzzled and intrigued.

The pilot, a skilled and seasoned aviator, reached behind his seat and retrieved a windshield cover. In a moment of uncertainty, he placed the cover over half of the windshield, shielding his side from the glaring sun. My initial confusion quickly turned to curiosity as I watched him rely on his instruments with unwavering confidence.

Intrigued, I questioned his decision upon landing. His response resonated deeply with me: "A skilled pilot trusts his instrumentation." He explained that flying is not just about sight but also about interpreting data, about relying on the science of flight to navigate safely.

Reflecting on this encounter, I couldn't help but draw parallels to life itself. In an age where intuition often reigns supreme, there is immense value in trusting the data, in making decisions grounded in empirical evidence rather than gut feelings.

As we navigate the complexities of our personal and professional lives, it's crucial to cultivate reliable systems and processes—our own instrumentation—to guide us. Whether in

business or in relationships, the ability to access and interpret data empowers us to make informed decisions and chart a course towards success.

In the words of the legendary Jay-Z, "Men lie, women lie, numbers don't." Building robust systems that provide us with accurate data enables us to see beyond the surface and make sound judgments.

So, as we journey forward, let us embrace the wisdom of trusting the instrumentation. May we cultivate the tools and insights needed to navigate life's challenges with clarity and confidence.

Cheers, and here's to a future guided by data-driven decisions. Thank you.

Chapter 13:

Curating Your Information Intake

In the whirlwind of modern communication, it's easy to feel overwhelmed by the sheer volume of messages inundating our inboxes and social media accounts. Over the past couple of days, I've had numerous encounters with individuals expressing frustration at the lack of response to their messages. Allow me to shed some light on the situation.

In the digital realm, I'm bombarded with thousands of messages across various platforms. On LinkedIn alone, my inbox is flooded with over 6,000 messages, with a significant portion residing in the often neglected "InMail" section. Additionally, my email accounts collectively receive upwards of 250 emails daily. Instagram, another hub of interaction, sees an average of 30 direct messages sliding into my inbox each day. And let's not forget Facebook, where the message count easily surpasses 200 on a daily basis.

Navigating this deluge of communication is akin to traversing a dense forest without a map. Each message, ranging from brief inquiries to lengthy essays, demands attention and consideration. However, the reality is that the sheer volume prohibits thorough individual responses.

Consider this scenario: You compose a detailed message, pouring your thoughts and inquiries onto the digital page. But amidst the sea of messages flooding my inbox, yours risks being lost in the tide. It's not a matter of negligence or disregard; it's simply a logistical challenge.

Yet, amidst this digital cacophony, there lies an opportunity for refinement and efficiency. It begins with a conscious effort to curate the content we consume. Just as we select our meals carefully to nourish our bodies, we must choose our information sources thoughtfully to nourish our minds.

First and foremost, prioritize industry-specific information. Whether you're a garment manufacturer or a tech entrepreneur, staying abreast of developments in your field is paramount. Subscribe to industry newsletters, join associations, and engage with relevant online communities to access timely insights.

Secondly, cultivate a repository of motivational content. Platforms like Goalcast offer a treasure trove of inspirational videos and stories to uplift and energize. Feed your spirit with positivity and resilience, especially during moments of doubt or fatigue.

Lastly, engage in continuous learning. Just as physical exercise keeps our bodies fit, intellectual stimulation keeps our minds agile. Enroll in courses, attend seminars, or embark on a self-directed learning journey. Challenge yourself to explore new ideas and perspectives regularly.

In essence, take charge of your information intake. Be discerning in what you consume, seeking sources that enrich and empower you. And for those seeking to connect with influencers or industry leaders, consider alternative avenues beyond direct messaging. A well-crafted introduction or a mutual connection can often pave the way for meaningful dialogue.

So, as we navigate the digital landscape, let's strive for clarity amidst the noise. By curating our information intake with purpose and intention, we empower ourselves to thrive in an age of information abundance.

Chapter 14:

Making Decisions Based on Data

The hardest decision to make about something you're emotionally invested in is to remove your emotion and make decisions based on the data. It's a struggle all of us have. At what point do you remove your emotion from making a decision and make the decision purely based on the data?

The reason this is difficult is because, as human beings, we live in a world of emotion. We feel, we love, we hurt, we hate, we project our own prejudices, and we are socialized in a particular way. We fall in love, start businesses because of our passions, and pursue specific careers because we're gifted and passionate about them. But at a certain point in our growth journey, decisions have to be based on the data.

One of the hardest things to learn about your growth and evolution cycle is that certain things that work earlier on may no longer serve you when you want to move to the next level. Learning the difference and how to change your own disposition when the environment around you changes is fundamental. Learning how to remove your own emotion and approach things looking at the facts and data is crucial.

So how do you remove the emotion? That's the hard part. Most of us struggle with it. When I was younger, I used to do martial arts and attended training camps where there was no hot water. I questioned why we kept going to a place without hot water, only to learn that they did have it, but we were instructed to turn it off. It was a deliberate exercise to train our minds to conquer our bodies.

Training your mind to conquer your body is a fundamental part of the growth process because the decisions you need to make require you to exist outside of emotion; they need to be driven by facts, not feelings. One way to muster your emotions is to extract yourself from the situation and view it as a third party giving advice. This shift in perspective can be transformative.

To make data-based decisions, you need to differentiate between good data and bad data. Bad data often comes with distortion or bias in the way the question is framed. Therefore, asking the right question is crucial to obtaining good data. The question frames the data, so ensure that it reflects a real and good question.

Finally, making decisions based on data means leading with the business case. Ask yourself if the decision moves you closer to the desired outcome or if it feeds your ego, insecurities, or fears. Strive to make decisions that move you closer to your goals.

While making decisions based on data may feel unnatural at first, it's essential. Just like banks moved away from human biases in credit decisions by implementing credit scoring systems, you can implement systems in your life to remove emotions from important decisions. Whether it's seeking advice from mentors or having sponsors guide you, removing emotion and making decisions based on data will ultimately benefit you in the long run. Cheers.

Chapter 15:

The Legacy of Old Money

Thank you. Thank you. Thank you so much, Vusi. This particular episode is just everything. I personally look up to you, and just hearing you talk about the snowball effect has made me realize how I've gotten so engrossed with your result and I've not taken into consideration your process and the process of how you've got into this place, where you're in motivation and you have massive impacts to us and every one of us in the VT community. Thank you so much. This was such an eye-opener, and I personally would, you know, rededicate myself to the pursuit of why I want to be where I want to be. You really helped me. Thank you.

It's time to take your seat at the table, find out how with Vusi Tembeguayo as we discuss ideas that matter, a catalyst for bold action. Hello, family, and welcome to another episode of the VT podcast.

It feels so good to say that again, hello, family. First, a warm happy birthday to my little girl. Ama, daddy loves you so, so, so much. My daughter just turned 10 years old. She was very keen to remind me that now that she's double digits, she deserves a mobile phone, so Daddy has committed to doing it, and we'll certainly make sure that it happens. I had the most amazing, amazing, amazing time with the family and the kids and the birthday, and it just feels so good, and it fills my heart to live in a time where one is able to make sure that you can make your children's wildest dreams come true and to be blessed with the ability to make their dreams come true, as I think something none of us should ever take for granted, so happy birthday, memes and dreams.

As you guys would know, it was my birthday about three weeks ago, I turned 37 years old. I'm actually quite nervous about this age 37. It feels so mature, doesn't it when somebody says, "So, how old are you?" and you go, "I'm 37." You know it. Whatever you say after you say your age at 37 years old can't be immature. You've got to be structured, considered, you've got to be wise, and open to the world. Very excited to have reached this beautiful age of 37 years old this year. For the first time, I dedicated my birthday to being of service to others. So I spent the full day doing stuff that, in the right time, I'll tell you guys what we did, but we're very excited the team and I. But what we're able to do for the community on my 37th birthday this year and the 21st of March. I'm still accepting presents, by the way, so for those of you who would like to send us a gift or two, I'm open to receiving your presence. I also am very excited to share that we have finally launched Club 100. Yep, that's right! You heard it right. We finally launched the VT Club, 100, and I'm so excited. The uptake for the club 100 has been unbelievable. If you want to find out all about it, it's a private mentorship platform with me. You go to vtclub100.com, and you'll find out everything you need to find out about the club. Very excited to have you as part of the community. Right, friends and family, this week, I wanted to talk to you guys a bit about old money.

Old money moves differently. Now, I know that the correct English is "Old money moves differently," but it just has a bit more youth spunk, isn't it? It captures the zeitgeist of the lingua franca of how young people speak today when you say, "It moves different. Old money moves different." Less than a week ago, I was at a dinner with the family, the Lohner family, who run this incredible institution called Africa Token. They do a lot of work in South

Africa, specifically to help the development of communities. They're very embedded in communities, deep in Alexandra. They find young people from previously disadvantaged backgrounds. In truth, most of them from presently disadvantaged backgrounds, and they give them a fair shot at life. They equip them with life skills and job opportunities and a whole host of things that, frankly, were not for them in the work that they do. Those young people would be much poorer for it, let alone probably not included in the mainstream economy. So I was delivering the keynote at this particular event, and I had a fantastic time. We reflected a lot about where South Africa finds itself. And even though I'm a global citizen and I live in other parts of the world, South Africa, for me, is still home. I still have businesses in South Africa, so I'm very tethered to what's happening in South Africa, even though, to be completely honest with you, I would sometimes prefer it not to be so. So we had this evening. It's a fantastic evening in this dinner. You know, the three-course dinners, the starters.

I'll never forget the very first time I had starters was in the year 2004. Listen to this, and I was speaking at the Black Management Forum event at what was then Caesar's Palace in Boksburg. The South Africans would know that today it's called Emperors. And by the way, in fact, for calling it Caesar's, you show your age. And the Black

Management Forum was celebrating 10 years of empowerment, 1994-2004. It was my first professional paying public speaking gig. And it was the first time in my life I had starters. I didn't know about starters until then. So when they said to us they were serving, and they brought this little entree with food in it, I thought, "Well, this is not going to be filling." And that was the first time I ever had starters, anyway. So we had this event, this beautiful event over the past week, great meals, etc. And then toward the end of the event, I start and come upon a conversation with a gentleman who, for the purposes of this podcast, will remain unnamed. But he is at the helm of controlling the endowment fund of one of the wealthiest families on the continent, the Sundarman Fund, by the way. Numbers in the tens of millions of dollars. It's a substantial endowment fund, and he controls the fund right now. I know of the fund because being in the fund management space, which I am, and from the institutional investors we raise from, the name of the fund has come up a couple of times as a provider of soft capital to create anchor in your fund so that you can raise from the institutions. So I know of the fund, but I didn't know him anyway.

So I get to meet him. We started chatting. I tell him a bit about what we're doing. We're right in the middle of a fundraising program. As some of you in this podcast know, we're raising

Chapter 16:

The Demise of Heroes

If there's something I can't give you in exchange for everything you give to me, it's the memory of heroes who once walked among us. I grew up in a time where the concept of a "full room" meant exactly that, not a euphemism for luxurious living. In those apartheid-style houses, every street seemed to host its own makeshift economy - a hair salon here, a puzzle shop there, and always a spot for clandestine drinks and camaraderie. These were the haunts of everyday heroes, the unsung entrepreneurs who carved out livelihoods from meager beginnings.

Hello, everyone. We wanted to take some time today to address a question that's been weighing heavily on my mind: Where have all the black heroes gone? I remember a time when our community boasted men and women of remarkable achievement, individuals we could look up to with pride. But somewhere along the way, we've lost sight of these beacons of inspiration, replacing celebration with condemnation.

When I was a child, I idolized figures like Jabu Stone and Dr. Herman Mashaba, whose entrepreneurial spirit blazed a trail for others to follow. These were the heroes who showed us what was possible, who made us believe that success was within reach. But today, it seems we've traded admiration for scrutiny, tearing down those who dare to rise above the fray.

In other communities, I've witnessed a different approach to success. A sense of communal responsibility, a commitment to uplift those who stumble and support those who strive. It's a concept encapsulated in the Yiddish word "fargin," a reminder that we are stronger together, that our collective success depends on lifting each other up.

But here, in our own community, we've succumbed to a culture of tearing down rather than building up. We've vilified our heroes, reduced them to mere mortals with flaws to exploit. And in doing so, we've robbed our youth of role models, of dreams to aspire to, of hope for a brighter future.

I've seen the headlines, the gleeful pronouncements of downfall and defeat. But behind those words are real people, with real struggles and real dreams. People like Aliko Dangote, whose ambition and drive have propelled him to great heights, only to be met with derision and scorn.

We must ask ourselves: What do we stand to gain by tearing down our heroes? What does it say about us as a community, as a society? Perhaps it's time to reassess our judgments, to recognize that heroes are not infallible beings, but flawed individuals striving for excellence in their own way.

So to those who would revel in the downfall of others, I urge you to consider the impact of your words. And to those who continue to build, to dream, to strive against the odds, I salute you. You are the true heroes, the ones who inspire us to reach for greatness.

This video is dedicated to you, the unsung heroes of our community. Keep going, keep striving, for someday, the world will recognize the greatness within you.

Thank you for watching. Don't forget to subscribe to the channel and leave a comment below. Until next time, take care.

Chapter 17:

Surrendering to the Flow

It's actually easier than you think. The calling on your life was imprinted long before you took your first breath, before you entered this world in flesh and blood. Your destiny was etched in the annals of history. Thus, living your life becomes an experiment in faith.

It's about acknowledging that there's a purpose guiding your journey and embracing that path. Following your calling is simpler than you imagine. My mantra for this year is "flow, not force." If something feels rushed, I slow down. I seek spaces and connections that align with my natural rhythm, rather than resisting it.

Far too often, we find ourselves clinging to relationships, careers, and situations that no longer serve us. We force outcomes instead of allowing the natural course of life to unfold. But there's a wisdom in surrendering to the flow of life.

In the early stages, it's challenging. We crave control, certainty, and predictability. But true growth lies in relinquishing that control and trusting in the universe's plan. Letting go of what we know, even if it means uncertainty and discomfort, is the essence of embracing flow.

What is the flow of your life? Yesterday, during a master class with the VT Club 100 group, we delved into this question. Members shared their journeys of transitioning from force to flow, realizing that operating in alignment with their calling was far more fulfilling than merely tapping into their capacities.

Flow isn't about doing what you can; it's about doing what you must. It's about embracing your calling, even if it defies conventional paths or societal expectations. Finding your flow means aligning with your purpose, not just your capabilities.

So, I encourage you to reflect on your life's calling. Embrace the resistance, for it is often a sign that you're on the right path. The journey may not be easy, but it will be worth it. Surrender to the flow, and you'll find a depth of fulfillment that force can never achieve.

As we embark on this journey together, remember: Your challenges are not obstacles; they are indicators of your calling. Have the courage to pursue your destiny with patience, resilience, and faith in the flow of life.

Wishing you all an extraordinary week ahead. Stay true to your calling, and may the flow guide you to greatness.

**Conclusion:

As we come to the end of this transformative journey, I am reminded of the profound wisdom that has unfolded within these pages. Throughout this book, we have explored the depths of human experience, delving into the complexities of life, love, purpose, and resilience.

From the earliest chapters to the final pages, one theme echoes resoundingly: the power of embracing the journey. Life is not a destination but a winding path filled with twists, turns, and unexpected detours. It is in navigating these challenges that we discover our true strength and potential.

At the heart of our exploration lies the essence of authenticity. We have peeled back the layers of societal expectations and personal insecurities to uncover the raw beauty of our true selves. In doing so, we have found liberation and empowerment, recognizing that our uniqueness is our greatest gift.

But this journey has not been solitary. Along the way, we have encountered fellow travelers—kindred spirits whose stories have intertwined with our own. Through shared experiences and mutual support, we have forged connections that transcend the boundaries of time and space.

Yet, amidst the triumphs and joys, we have also encountered moments of darkness and doubt. We have faced fears, setbacks, and moments of uncertainty. But through it all, we have persevered, drawing upon the reservoirs of courage and resilience that lie within each of us.

As we reflect on the chapters of this book, let us carry forward the lessons learned and the wisdom gained. Let us embrace each new day with a spirit of curiosity and wonder, knowing that every experience, whether joyful or challenging, is a stepping stone on the path to growth.

May we approach life with open hearts and open minds, embracing the beauty of imperfection and the richness of diversity. And may we never forget that the true essence of our journey lies not in reaching a destination, but in savoring each precious moment along the way.

As the final page turns, let us embark on the next chapter of our lives with courage, grace, and gratitude. For in the end, it is not the destination that defines us, but the journey itself—and the indelible mark we leave upon the world.

Farewell, dear reader, and may your journey be filled with love, laughter, and boundless possibilities.

www.ingramcontent.com/pod-product-compliance
Lightning Source LLC
Chambersburg PA
CBHW062115220526
45471CB00010B/3749